4/93

P9-ECL-699

LOOKING AT PAINTINGS

Families

The Guillon-Lethiere Family, 1815
Jean-Auguste-Dominique Ingres, French (1780–1867)

LOOKING AT PAINTINGS

Families

Peggy Roalf

Series Editor
Jacques Lowe

Designer
Amy Hill

Hyperion Books for Children

A
JACQUES LOWE
VISUAL ARTS PROJECTS
BOOK

Text Copyright © 1992 by Jacques Lowe Visual Arts Projects Inc.
A Jacques Lowe Visual Arts Projects Book

Printed in Italy

FIRST EDITION

1 3 5 7 9 10 8 6 4 2

LIBRARY OF CONGRESS CATALOGING-IN-PUBLICATION DATA
Roalf, Peggy.
Families/Peggy Roalf — 1st ed.
p. cm. — (Looking at paintings)
"A Jacques Lowe Visual Arts projects book" — T.p. verso.
Includes bibliographical references and index.
Summary: Presents 2,000 years of art history through a series of
family portraits and paintings of family scenes.
ISBN: 1-56282-087-7 (trade) — ISBN: 1-56282-088-5 (lib. bdg.)
1. Family in art — Juvenile literature. 2. Painting — Juvenile
literature. [1. Family in art. 2. Painting — History. 3. Art
appreciation.] I. Title. II. Series: Roalf, Peggy. Looking at paintings.
ND1460.F34R6 1992
757 — dc20   91–73830
CIP
AC

Contents

Introduction

*L*OOKING AT PAINTINGS is a series of books about understanding what great artists see when they paint. Painters have been attracted to the subject of family life for more than three thousand years. Some artists have painted loving portraits of their own families. Others have looked at everyday life and special occasions in other homes—from a poor farm in Haiti to a great castle in Spain. By looking at many pictures of families, we see how artists use their talent and imagination to create a personal view of this subject.

Painters are creative explorers. They search their own feelings to show us something about each family group—affection, pride, and, sometimes, anger. They often create an unusual mood or a unique setting through the use of color, design, and light. With their singular power of observation, painters can find something special in everything they see and often invent radical painting techniques to express a personal vision.

We will see that Andrea Mantegna created the illusion of soaring space in an ordinary room with a flat ceiling, in *Family and Court of Ludovico III Gonzaga*. Claude Monet used bold yellow and blue highlights to create the atmosphere of outdoor light around his future wife, Camille, in *Luncheon on the Grass*. In *Hommage à Louis David*, Fernand Léger used stinging colors and industrial forms to express the influence of modern technology on everyday life.

Artists transform what they see into magical images that take us on a journey to other times and to distant places. You can learn to observe your own family—in everyday activities and on special occasions—and use your imagination to see like a painter.

FAMILY SCENE, about 1150 B.C.
Tomb of Inherkhan, Dier el Medineh, Thebes
Unknown Egyptian artist, Watercolor on plaster (detail)

For wealthy Egyptians in ancient times, life on earth was so good they hoped that life after death would be exactly the same. Their tombs consisted of elaborate rooms covered with wall paintings that were pictorial messages to the gods, almost like a map to everlasting life.

Egyptian artists painted figures to show not only what they saw before them but also what they *knew was there*. The head and the body from the waist to the feet are painted in profile, whereas the upper part of the body and the eye are shown straight on. A hand holding an object is usually drawn so that we can see all of the fingers. Egyptian artists, like those in other ancient cultures, drew important people larger than the less important ones. In this painting, the servant is much smaller than the mother, father, and older son. She wears no jewelry and is painted entirely in profile.

This unusual way of painting the human figure was essential to the burial ceremony. Because none of the important parts of the body is hidden from view, the figure in the painting represents the whole person. When a priest touched a figure in the painting with a staff, he gave that person eternal life. Objects were treated in a similar way: A platter of figs is painted as though seen from above to display each piece of fruit. When the Egyptian's soul awakens, there will be something good to eat. The dead were provided with everything they needed for the next life—family, delicious food, and enjoyable activities.

Young children in ancient Egypt did not wear clothes because of the heat, but they had elaborate hairstyles and beautiful jewelry.

FAMILY AND COURT OF LUDOVICO III GONZAGA, 1474
Andrea Mantegna, Italian (1431–1506), Fresco (detail)

The Marchese Ludovico Gonzaga of Mantua acquired gold and land by defeating his enemies in Venice and Milan. In 1459, he decided to devote more of his time and wealth to politics and family life. Ludovico hired Andrea Mantegna to be his official painter. Mantegna began the task of glorifying the

The fireplace is real, but the high arched ceiling is an illusion created by Mantegna.

Gonzaga palace with frescoes such as this one in which the family awaits the return of the oldest son, Francesco, who has just been made a cardinal of the Roman Catholic church.

Andrea Mantegna had to decide in advance exactly how his paintings would look because in fresco the artist paints directly onto wet plaster, which dries quickly. First he made a full-size drawing called a cartoon, named for the kind of heavy paper used, which was known as *cartone*. Mantegna then transferred the drawing onto the wall and applied a thin layer of fresh plaster only to the area that he could complete in one session. He had to work boldly, quickly, and carefully all at the same time. Even with the limitations of fresco painting, he achieved delicate effects in the individual portraits and in the details of the luxurious clothing.

Mantegna used a painting technique known as *trompe l'oeil*, which means "to fool the eye." The larger-than-life-size figures seem to be stepping out of a small terrace into the palace room. Notice that the marchese's right foot and the hem of the marchesa's dress appear to project beyond the floor of the terrace where they sit.

PORTRAIT OF THE EMPEROR MAXIMILIAN I AND HIS FAMILY, 1515

Bernhard Strigel, German (1460–1528), On wood, 28½" x 23⅝"

By the time Maximilian I became the Holy Roman Emperor in 1493, the title had lost most of its importance. He was poor for an emperor, but that did not prevent him from bringing talented painters to his court.

Bernhard Strigel came from a family of successful painters and wood carvers who created religious art for churches, but his special talent was portrait painting. In this picture, Strigel portrays the emperor; his first wife, Mary of Burgundy; their eldest son, Philip; Philip's two sons; and a grandson-in-law. Maximilian commissioned this painting to celebrate the double wedding of his grandsons in 1515.

To please the emperor, Strigel created a highly finished surface that looks like enamel. Among Strigel's other trademarks were his use of richly brocaded cloth in the background and an open window with a dreamlike imaginary landscape in the distance. The Latin text was added by a later owner who attempted to give this painting religious meaning.

Strigel was one of the first artists to create more casual portraits at a time when most portraits were stiff and serious pictures of important people or biblical scenes created for churches. Instead of looking straight out at the viewer, the emperor and his family converse and show affection. Paintings such as this, which showed the personality and not just the appearance of the sitter, became known as *character portraits*.

CLEOPHAS FRATER CARNALIS IO=
SEPHI MARITI DIVAE VIRG NAPIAE

I
JACOBVS MINOR FPVS·   MARIA CLEOPHÆ SOROR
HIEROSOLIMITANVS· VIRG MAR PVTATIVA MA
TERTERA D· N·

III   II
IOSEPH IVSTVS SIMON ZELOTES CONSO=
BRINVS DNI NRI

13

RUBENS, HIS WIFE HELENA FOURMENT AND THEIR SON PETER PAUL, about 1639

Peter Paul Rubens, Flemish (1577–1640), Oil on panel, 80⅜" x 62⅝"

Peter Paul Rubens had a long and triumphant career creating paintings for many of the kings and queens of Europe. He lived at a time when death at an early age was common; by 1626 he had lost his first wife and three of his five beloved children. Four years later, when he was fifty-three years old, he married sixteen-year-old Hélèna Fourment and began to raise a second family.

Rubens studied a different pose for his wife, Hélèna, in this pencil drawing.

Rubens filled this portrait with things that had personal meaning. He chose the elegant Spanish-style clothing to show respect for King Philip IV of Spain, a patron for whom Rubens created many masterpieces. The garden design hints at his enjoyment of antiques, and an overflowing fountain represents Rubens's appreciation of Hélèna's youth and beauty.

By emphasizing Hélèna's pearly skin tones, Rubens made her gesture and young Peter Paul's response the focus of the painting. A brilliant red parrot among the roses directs our eyes to the mother and child, while Rubens stands back, at the side, gazing lovingly at his wife.

Rubens made the people in his paintings come alive through his masterful technique for creating skin tones. He started with a neutral, grayish tone and added shadows in the early stages of painting. Rubens then created the luminous flesh tones by applying transparent and semitransparent colored glazes over the neutral underpainting, allowing the layers to dry in between. As a finishing touch, he painted glowing, opaque white highlights.

In this very personal, life-size portrait, Rubens created a love letter to his family.

THE MAIDS OF HONOR, 1656

Diego Rodríguez de Silva Velázquez, Spanish (1599–1660),
Oil on canvas, 126" x 111"

Velázquez was an apprentice artist at the age of eleven and a master painter at nineteen. He was an ambitious man who knew that his artistic genius made him an equal among the nobles of the Spanish court.

Philip IV became king of Spain when he was eighteen years old, in 1621. Two years later, he chose Velázquez to be one of several royal artists. Close in age, they formed a friendship that lasted the rest of Velázquez's life. Philip loved his family and his great art collection, but he was a failure as a king. Spain lost its glory and wealth during his reign and came dangerously close to civil war.

Velázquez also held the post of king's chamberlain, the most important position in the palace. His work as a court official robbed time from painting—in his forty-year career, Velázquez created fewer than one hundred twenty-five

Velázquez portrayed himself as a proud and accomplished man wearing the red cross of Santiago, the emblem of knighthood.

canvases. Velázquez was rewarded in 1658, when Philip honored him with a knighthood.

The Maids of Honor draws us into Velázquez's life at the Alcázar Palace. The Infanta Margarita has posed for the artist many times before, but today the princess is restless. Two young maids of honor, Maria and Isabel, try to quiet her. The dwarf Maribárbola (one of Margarita's playmates) glares at us, and Nicolás, another dwarf, kicks the napping hound. Velázquez is dressed in the fine clothes of a nobleman and he steps back from his enormous canvas to look straight out at us. At first, it seems that we are the subject of his painting in progress.

When we look closely at this painting, we notice two more people. The king and queen are reflected in a mirror at the end of the dark room. Will they be part of Velázquez's painting, whose surface is hidden from view, or are they just visiting their daughter?

Velázquez created the illusion of a great space by painting many different kinds of light. Sunshine pours in through a tall window at the right, flooding the foreground. A shadowy area with dimly lit figures in the middle of the picture is followed by another tall window spilling in just enough light to reveal the mirror reflecting the king and queen's image. A door in the back wall opens to another brightly lit room. To make the islands of light sparkle in contrast, Velázquez painted greenish gray tones all around.

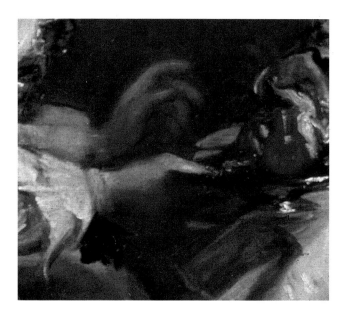

This detail shows the soft painting technique Velázquez used to create the appearance of movement.

Velázquez modeled the faces of the infanta and her companions with delicacy. But their hands are painted as flutters of movement rather than precisely described fingers. Velázquez painted bold blotches of black, red, and white over the silver of Margarita's gown. On top of these shimmering masses of color, he used fine brush strokes to indicate the ribbon and lace.

Even though *The Maids of Honor* looks so real that we feel we could join the group, Velázquez has also created an air of mystery. In this picture of great riches, he painted the king and queen as ghostly images in a distant mirror. We sense their presence, but we also sense their faded glory.

19

THE BRIDGES FAMILY, 1804
John Constable, English (1776–1837), Oil on canvas, 53½" x 72⅜"

John Constable was born in the first year of the American Revolution and lived at a time of global expansion, when personal success was prized. But Constable preferred the English countryside of his childhood to big cities and foreign travel. He wanted to express the beauty of the natural world by painting landscapes, but like other artists, he painted portraits to survive.

George Bridges was a successful merchant who commissioned Constable to paint a family portrait. Constable took the assignment and did something completely unexpected. He brought the warm feeling of the landscape through an open window into the living room. Constable re-created the transparent flickering light from the sky on the dresses of Mrs. Bridges and her daughters; the glowing colors of the sunset brighten their faces. The dark clothing of Mr. Bridges and his sons echoes the color of the distant trees. Instead of creating a room filled with luxurious decorations, Constable painted what was important to him—the changing, natural light.

Constable painted *The Bridges Family* with the same kind of bold brush strokes and rough textures that he used in his landscape paintings. It seemed crude compared to the polished portraits that were popular at the time.

This was one of the last portraits Constable ever created. He continued painting landscapes and teaching, but his work was never appreciated in England during his lifetime.

Thomas Gainsborough, another celebrated English painter, lived a half century before Constable. In his drawing of a family group, he created the effect of soft light through the use of black and white chalk on rough-textured paper.

THE BELLELLI FAMILY, 1858–67

Edgar Degas, French (1834–1917), Oil on canvas, 78 3/4" x 98 3/8"

*E*dgar Degas created an unusual group portrait when he painted his favorite aunt, Laura Bellelli; her husband, Baron Gennaro Bellelli; and their children. Looking at this painting, we can feel a great sadness. The family was in the process of a divorce.

The baroness is dressed entirely in black; she stands protectively over her daughter Giovanna, who looks unhappily out at the viewer. At the center, Giulia casually sits with one foot tucked up, but with her arms in an impatient pose, her face the younger image of her sad mother's. With his back to the viewer, the baron looks away from his reading, but not at his family. All four seem to be remote from each other.

Degas increased the tense feeling in this scene by using colors, patterns, and light. The children's crisp white pinafores make the large areas of black in the painting seem even blacker. Soft patterns in the carpet and wallpaper give a feeling of comfort in contrast to the family's discomfort. Degas adds a chilly note to the scene with light reflecting from a mirror above the unlighted fireplace.

Edgar Degas did not paint this portrait to please his relatives. He was twenty-four years old when he began this painting and was trying to gain public recognition with a picture so large it would be noticed. Instead of creating a painting of nations at war — a popular theme with artists at the time — he showed the private drama of a troubled family.

In this detail, we can see the strength of Laura Bellelli's protective hand and the softness of her daughter's young hands.

LUNCHEON ON THE GRASS, 1866
Claude Monet, French (1840–1926), Oil on canvas, 97⅝" x 96⅛"

Claude Monet was amazed by the magical way that sunlight and shadows could change the appearance of colors. In 1865, he spent the summer painting in a forest, to see and feel the color of natural light. Monet's future wife, Camille Doncieux, and his good friend Frédéric Bazille were his models. Working outdoors, Monet painted small studies, which he later used to create this painting of life-size figures at a leisurely picnic.

Monet solved a technical problem and developed a new painting method in this early work. Ready-made paints, in tubes, had been available since 1841. They made working outdoors easier, but the linseed oil in the paint turned light colors yellow. Monet soaked out the unwanted oil with blotter paper, then added poppy oil and lead white paint, which did not yellow.

Using large brushes, Monet painted slabs of bright, opaque colors and created the sensation of outdoor light and air. He painted light blue highlights—the color of the sky—on Bazille's suit. Monet lit up a platter of fruit with pale yellow brush strokes and painted lavender shadows on the white tablecloth to recreate the cool feeling of the forest.

Luncheon on the Grass was originally about fifteen by twenty feet. To pay the rent, Monet gave the painting to his landlord, who put it in a damp cellar and forgot it. Several years later, when Monet could afford to buy back the canvas, it had rotted. He cut off and saved this section—and displayed it in his studio for the rest of his life.

In a close-up detail, we can see the bold yellow and blue highlights, which blend together when seen from far away.

FAMILY REUNION, 1865–69
Jean-Frédéric Bazille, French (1841–70), Oil on canvas, 60" x 91½"

*J*ean-Frédéric Bazille came from a prosperous family of wine growers and studied medicine to please his mother and father. Bazille was also a talented painter who spent much of his time with his friends Edouard Manet; Edgar Degas; Pierre-Auguste Renoir; and Claude Monet, with whom he shared a studio. When Bazille failed medical school in 1864, his family understood his passion for art, and they backed him.

The year after Bazille had posed for Monet's painting *Luncheon on the Grass*, he used the same subject as Monet—stylish people in an outdoor setting—to create a formal portrait of his beloved family.

Bazille focused on the people, not the landscape, and created a dramatic scene. We almost feel like intruders when we look at this painting. Bazille's relatives seem suspended in time, as though interrupted during an intimate conversation. Bazille is also there, looking out from behind his uncle, on the left.

Family Reunion, 1865–69

The trees and distant hills seem as flat as scenery in a play; the light on his cousin Therèse, turning in her chair, resembles artificial, theatrical lighting; the hat and bouquet of flowers are like props at the front of a stage.

In 1868, Frédéric Bazille's success seemed certain when *Family Reunion* was selected for an important exhibition in Paris. But one year later, Bazille was killed on the battlefield during the Franco-Prussian War. Although he created fewer than sixty paintings, Bazille's talent was publicly recognized, and he is remembered for the friendship and financial support he gave to fellow artists.

THE MONET FAMILY IN THEIR GARDEN, 1874
Edouard Manet, French (1832–83), Oil on canvas, 24" x 39½"

"Every time I paint, I throw myself into the water in order to learn how to swim," said Edouard Manet. He believed that there was not just one "right" way to paint, but many. So, Manet reinvented the art of painting every time he faced a blank canvas. In 1874, he painted outdoors for the first time with his friends Claude Monet and Pierre-Auguste Renoir. Manet created this picture in appreciation of their great friendship.

Manet's painting of the Monet family seems to sparkle with *many* colors. A close look shows that Manet actually achieved this effect by using very *few* colors. Madame Monet's dress is a block of pale pink, with overlays of gray and a darker pink to suggest details. Manet used the same shade of pink in the sky beyond the grove of trees. Both Monet's shirt and his son Jean's clothes are the same blue, but Manet added transparent patches of white over the boy's suit to indicate touches of sunlight. He created shadows by adding blue paint to the green of the grass and trees and splashed sketchy red shapes for the flowers along three sides of the garden.

With the strong contrast of bright red against quiet green paint, Manet has created the illusion of many colors and the atmosphere of a cool spring morning. Manet painted the same red on Jean's hat, in Madame Monet's fan, and on the rooster's comb to focus our attention on the Monet family—and on the family of curious chickens.

Pierre-Auguste Renoir often used his family and friends as models. Renoir drew his friend Edouard Manet's niece, Julie, using black crayon on rough-textured paper.

MADAME CHARPENTIER AND HER CHILDREN, GEORGETTE AND PAUL, 1878

Pierre-Auguste Renoir, French (1841–1919), Oil on canvas, 60 ½" x 74 ⅞"

This portrait was Renoir's first important commission, and he gave Madame Charpentier all that she could wish for in a painting. Her husband was the publisher of books by France's greatest authors, including Emile Zola and Gustave Flaubert. Georges Charpentier spoiled his family with the luxuries of life, and his wife wears her happiness like precious jewelry. Renoir captured the splendid antiques, golden scrolls, and beautiful crystal in Madame Charpentier's Japanese-style parlor. In this extravagant setting, the mother, her daughter, Georgette, young son, Paul, and even the dog are comfortably at home.

Renoir captured the gestures and expressions of a close, happy family when he painted a portrait of his wife and children.

A porcelain painter before he became a fine artist, Renoir developed a sure eye for details and a talent for painting luminous skin tones. The room is busy with patterns and shapes, but Renoir painted a large, pale yellow carpet that leads our eyes directly to the family. By repeating the red, the blue, and the greenish gold of the wall in most of the furnishings, Renoir unified the background and made the figures stand out. He created the luxurious effect of finely painted porcelain, but on a grand scale.

In nineteenth-century Paris, the only way for an artist to be successful was to have his work accepted in official exhibitions, which were known as "Salons." Renoir's family portrait was accepted by the Salon in April 1879. Madame Charpentier used her influence to ensure that the painting she so admired was prominently displayed, and Renoir's talent was publicly recognized for the first time.

PAUL HELLEU SKETCHING WITH HIS WIFE, 1889
John Singer Sargent, American (1856–1925), Oil on canvas, 26" x 32"

John Singer Sargent was a pilgrim of the arts. His family left the United States for Europe to see masterpieces of art in the great museums. It was a way of life, not a vacation—his mother wanted to give her family an exciting and rewarding life, and his father gave up a medical practice to support his wife's desire.

Sargent studied art in Paris when Edouard Manet, Pierre-Auguste Renoir, and Claude Monet were at the center of the art world. In 1887, he visited Monet at his country home. Sargent saw the master at work and admired Monet's visionary use of color. The following year, Sargent created this intimate portrait of his best friend from art school, Paul Helleu, with his bride, Alice Louise.

We can almost feel the misty atmosphere of a cool autumn day in this painting. Sargent balanced his colors *and* his brush strokes to create this effect. He painted the new family in neutral colors—gray, tan, and brown—with even strokes of the brush. He made the grass seem to shiver—dancing streaks of green paint shot with yellow and orange. Where the grass meets the water, it picks up cool, violet shadows.

In this picture, Sargent used all of the colors of the rainbow: red, orange, and yellow; blue, green, and violet. He balanced the bright red color of the canoe with the dull colors in the figures, the sharp green and yellow of the grass with the soft violet and blue of the shadows. This gives the painting an even, overall tone and shows Sargent's great understanding of the interaction of colors.

This detail shows that Sargent warmed the gray color of Alice Louise Helleu's blouse by mixing in the same red that he used for her lips—and for the canoe.

THE SCHUFFENECKER FAMILY, 1889
Paul Gauguin, French (1848–1903), Oil on canvas, 28 3/4" x 36 1/4"

Paul Gauguin saw life through his dreams and his memories. Observing an event, and sensing its emotional content, Gauguin looked for the most extreme lines, forms, and colors to convey his feelings. In his studio, he recalled these images and created a powerful expression of moments suspended in time.

The artist Emile Schuffenecker was Gauguin's closest friend for seventeen years. Often, when he could not pay his rent, Gauguin lived with the Schuffeneckers, who argued about his unpleasant and disruptive manner.

In this painting, Gauguin used extreme colors and shapes to create a disturbing atmosphere. A steep angle divides the room into two separate areas, and sharply drawn lines describe the tense figures of the adults. Emile occupies the blue zone; Madame Schuffenecker sits rigidly in the yellow zone with the unhappy children. Emile steps forward, as though to speak with his wife, but an easel blocks his way and shuts him into a corner. The brilliant red in the children's clothes creates another visual barrier between the parents.

Gauguin heightened the feeling of isolation in this painting by using strong, primary colors—red, yellow, and blue. The only softness is in the trees behind the barlike window supports. With bold lines and masses of intense color, Gauguin has conveyed the tension caused by a family quarrel.

Mary Cassatt, an American painter who lived in Paris, was captivated by the love between mothers and their children. She often exhibited her paintings with Gauguin, Monet, and Renoir.

THE FAMILY OF ACROBATS WITH APE, 1905
Pablo Picasso, Spanish (1881–1973),
Gouache, watercolor, and ink on cardboard, 41" x 29½"

The man who revolutionized modern art found his first success after he moved to Paris in 1904. Picasso was twenty-three years old and the leader of a group of painters and poets who struggled to make ends meet and still produce works of art. At night, they met in a local café to discuss their work and talk about life. When there was extra money, they often went to the theater.

Picasso's favorite entertainment was the circus, with its bareback riders, tumblers, and clowns. He sympathized with the poorly paid performers, whose offstage life was shabby compared to the glittering circus.

In this portrait, Picasso encloses a young circus family in a private world far away from the gaiety and noise of the ring. The range of rosy earth colors is as warm as this tender moment stolen between acts. Pale light and soft shadows enhance the intimate atmosphere. Even the ape, with its almost human expression, seems to reflect the closeness of circus life.

The parents' hands catch our eye. They are strong and wiry—strong enough to catch a flying acrobat, but soft enough to caress a baby. Picasso identifies himself—an artist who works magic in his paintings—with these performers who defy gravity in the circus ring.

Picasso saw his own life mirrored in the struggles and triumphs of this little family. He symbolized his optimism about the future in the active, healthy-looking baby. The gaunt parents represent the difficulties he had endured as a young painter.

Picasso expressed the young mother's complete devotion to her infant in this painting. The contrast between the dark clothing and the pale figures emphasized the mother's sheltering body.

PIANIST AND CHECKERS PLAYERS, 1924
Henri Matisse, French (1869–1954), Oil on canvas, 29" x 36⅜"

*H*enri Matisse was depressed by the misery caused by World War I. In Paris, food was scarce, winters were cold, and Matisse was exhausted by the difficulties of postwar life. In 1918, he left for Nice, in the south of France. There he found perfumed gardens—and a clear, silvery light that renewed his creativity.

The physical pleasure of painting, of working with glorious colors, made Matisse feel good. He captured his feeling of well-being in this painting of his richly decorated living room, where his daughter Marguerite plays the piano while his sons Pierre and Jean enjoy a game of checkers.

Matisse tilted the floor at a steep angle to spill the room out toward the viewer. Every square inch is covered with designs—flowers, rhythmic lines, and images of Matisse's paintings. He painted pattern on top of pattern. The black and white of the checkerboard is repeated as stripes on the boys' shirts, on the tablecloth, and on the edge of the carpet. The piano, a tall wardrobe, and a sideboard—plain, by comparison—define the sides of the room.

Matisse filled this painting with many shades of red—his *symbolic* color for light. And he also shows the *real* light of Nice by painting a silvery color on the back wall. A shadow cast by the sculpture tells us that there is a window to the right, beyond the edge of the picture.

The peace and harmony of this secluded room represent, in Henri Matisse's words, "a dream inspired by reality."

Matisse loved music and played the violin himself. He often painted his children while they practiced their lessons.

HOMMAGE A LOUIS DAVID, 1948–49
Fernand Léger, French (1881–1955), Oil on canvas, 60⅝" x 72⅞"

During World War II, Fernand Léger came to the United States and discovered an exciting new world in New York. He found a city transformed by machinery. Strong men operated powerful equipment to build skyscrapers, bridges, and subways. Flashing neon signs drenched the night in garish colors. Athletic women dressed in brightly colored shorts, like circus performers. To him, it was a completely unnatural world.

Back in France, Léger drew on these vivid images and his love of mechanical forms to create this painting of a family outing. The bicycles are like tubes; the men's arms and the fence, like pipes. The tubular tree on the left becomes a bicycle lock. Black shadows on the ground seem like sheet-metal cutouts. Even the foliage and the thick black outlines of the figures have a machine-made quality.

The women wear the kind of clothing Léger had seen in America: boldly patterned shorts in piercing colors, with cinch belts like metal bands. In contrast, the men seem oddly overdressed. Léger painted the figures straight on, like a blueprint. The figures overlap each other, but there seems to be no real space around them. Doves perched on little clouds seem to be pasted onto the artificial-looking sky, a flat mass of blue like a photographer's backdrop.

In his lifetime, Léger saw the world completely transformed by wars and by industrial progress. In this painting, he celebrated the positive effects of the machine age.

In this drawing of a mother and her son, Léger contrasted the soft pencil shading in the figures with the sharp edges of the window.

SIX STUDIES FOR FAMILY GROUP, 1948

Henry Moore, English (1898–1986), Pencil with wax crayon, watercolor, and ink, 20⅝" x 15¼"

Henry Moore's father was a coal miner. He spent long, grueling hours in the pits carving fuel from the rocks while his wife, Mary, struggled to care for their eight children. Like his father, Henry Moore also carved—but he became a sculptor who extracted his vision of life from great blocks of stone, often using the family group as his subject.

Creating sculpture is exhausting and time-consuming work. Every few months, Moore would put down his chisels to paint and draw. He said that drawing was a way to keep mentally fit—to feed his creativity and to develop ideas for new projects.

In this drawing, Moore divided his paper into six areas and studied different possibilities for a sculpture—the family with one child, with two children, in different poses, and seated on benches of various shapes. The simplified figures echo the forms of the ancient primitive sculpture he so much admired.

Moore began with wax crayons, then painted in watercolor. Using colored inks, he drew curved lines on the arms, legs, and heads. As he drew these "sectional lines," Moore mentally carved the figures of the parents into large sheltering forms. Highlights and dark tones create the effect of light and shadow. Moore was so practiced in drawing that he was able to draw rapidly and shape powerful images. But he believed that if he made highly finished drawings, his sculpture would suffer and look dull and lifeless.

Henry and Irina Moore's first child, Mary, was born in 1946. A devoted husband and father, Moore returned to the family group again and again, in drawing and in sculpture.

Henry Moore created blocks of color with large crayons to shape the child's figure and the parents' tender hands.

42

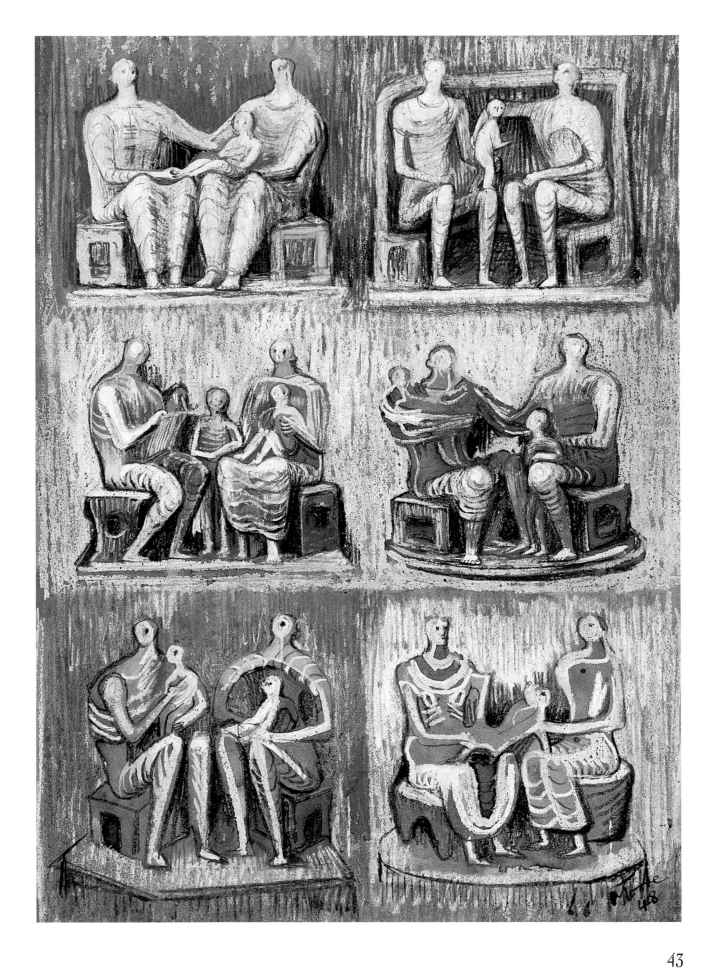

HAITIAN FAMILY, 1962
Castera Bazile, Haitian (1923–65), Oil on Masonite, 24" x 16"

Haiti has a proud history. In 1791, Toussaint-Louverture led a slave revolt against the French, and the first black republic in the world was established in 1804. But in the twentieth century, the country has been ruled by cruel dictators who have enriched themselves, forcing the peasants to live in desolation.

Castera Bazile realized his dream to be an artist in the capital city, Port-au-Prince. He developed his talent at the art center, where truck drivers, lawyers, and farmers painted together and exhibited their work. Bazile found inspiration in his African heritage, in Haitian folklore, and in everyday life.

In this family group, Bazile portrays the mother as an imposing figure, gently nursing her baby. Her husband holds his head in despair. The other child, deprived of the joys of youth, seems strangely old. The parents are too poor to buy shoes or clothes for the children.

The stillness of the mother's figure creates a visual contrast with angles and shapes that lead our eyes across the painting—angles in the father's arms, in the blank wall, in the soaring trunk of the tree.

Bazile used images and jewellike colors that have meaning in the Haitian voodoo religion. The child's red-and-white shirt is believed to protect against evil magic. Red and blue in the mother's clothes stand for warmth and strength. And the tree symbolizes a passageway to the spirit world, which offers the only relief from grinding poverty.

Jacques-Richard Chery, an artist who also worked at the Port-au-Prince Art Center, painted bold shapes and sharp angles in Mother and Child.

Glossary and Index

APPRENTICE, 16: A person who works for a master artist in exchange for training. In the seventeenth century, an apprentice's tasks included grinding pigments and preparing paints, mounting canvases onto frames, transferring the master's drawings onto canvas, and cleaning up the painting studio. After a long period of training, talented apprentices could become independent artists if they exhibited their works and captured the attention of patrons.

BACKGROUND, 12, 30: The part of a painting behind the subject; the distant area. (See FOREGROUND.)

Bazile, Castera, 44

Bazille, Jean-Frédéric (Pronounced Buh-zeel), 24, 26

Bellelli Family, The, 22

Bridges Family, The, 20

CANVAS, 16, 20, 22, 24, 26, 28, 30, 32, 34, 38, 40: A woven fabric (often linen or cotton) used as a painting surface. It is usually stretched tight and stapled onto a wooden frame in order to produce a flat, unwrinkled surface.

Cassatt, Mary, 34

CHARCOAL, 24, 28, 36: A soft black stick of burned wood, used to make drawings. Painters use charcoal because it can be blended and smudged, producing lines and tones of gray, as in a painting, but in black and white.

Chery, Jacques-Richard, 44

COMMISSION, 12, 20, 30: (1) A work of art produced at the request of a wealthy patron. (2) The appointment of an artist to create such a work of art.

Constable, John, 20

CONTRAST, 18, 22, 28, 36, 40, 44: Big differences in light and dark, shapes, colors, and activity.

Degas, Edgar (Pronounced Deh-gah), 22, 26

DESIGN, 14, 38: (1) The arrangement of objects and figures in a painting through the combination of colors and shapes. This is also called composition. (2) A pattern of shapes on a surface.

DETAIL, 8, 10, 18, 22, 24, 28, 30, 32, 42: (1) Small parts of a painting, such as objects on a table or decorations on a dress. (2) When used in a book: a section of a painting enlarged to provide a close-up view of textures and colors.

DRAWING, 10, 14, 20, 28, 40, 42: The art of creating an image by making marks on paper. Drawings can be made using dry materials such as pencil, charcoal, and crayon or wet materials such as ink and paint. Drawings may consist of lines, tones, shading, and dots. Twentieth-century artists began to create drawings that are difficult to distinguish from paintings. An important difference is that drawings are usually on paper rather than canvas, wood, or metal. Drawings produced with more than one kind of material are known as "mixed media" drawings.

ENAMEL, 12: (1) A glaze made of powdered colored glass, applied to metal and baked, or "fired," at a high temperature to produce a lustrous surface. (2) A paint that has a shiny, smooth surface when it dries.

Family and Court of Ludovico III Gonzaga, 7, 10

Family of Acrobats with Ape, The, 36

Family Reunion, 26

Family Scene, 8

FOREGROUND, 18: The area in a painting closest to the viewer. (See BACKGROUND.)

FRESCO, 10: A method of painting onto wet plaster, usually with watercolor, to create a picture in which the paint is absorbed into the wall instead of remaining on the surface.

Gainsborough, Thomas, 20

Gauguin, Paul (Pronounced Go-gann), 34

GLAZE, 14: A transparent, or almost transparent, thinned-down layer of paint applied over dry paint, allowing the colors underneath to show through.

Haitian Family, 44

HIGHLIGHT, 14, 24, 42: The lightest color or brightest white in a painting.

Hommage à Louis David, 7, 40

INK, 36, 42: Usually, a jet-black fluid made of powdered carbon mixed with a water-soluble liquid. Ink drawings can be made with dark lines and diluted tones of gray. Inks are also made in colors and used in paintings.

Léger, Fernand (Pronounced Leh-zheh), 7, 40

Luncheon on the Grass, 7, 24

Madame Charpentier and Her Children, Georgette and Paul, 30

Maids of Honor, The, 16

Manet, Edouard, 26, 28, 32

Mantegna, Andrea, 7, 10

Matisse, Henri, 38

Monet, Claude, 7, 24, 26, 28, 32

Monet Family in Their Garden, The, 28

Moore, Henry, 42

OPAQUE, 14, 24: Not letting light pass through. Opaque paints conceal what is under them. (The opposite of Transparent.)

PAINT: Artists have used different kinds of paint, depending on the materials that were available to them and the effects they wished to produce in their work.

Different kinds of paint are similar in the way they are made.

1. Paint is made by combining finely powdered pigment with a vehicle. A vehicle is a substance that evenly disperses the color and produces a consistency that can be like mayonnaise and sometimes as thick as peanut butter. The kind of vehicle used sometimes gives the paint its name. Pigment is the raw material that gives paint its color. Pigments are made from natural minerals and from man-made chemical compounds.

2. Paint is made thinner or thicker with a substance called a medium. Different paints require the use of mediums appropriate to their composition.

3. A solvent must be used by the painter to clean the paint from brushes, tools, and the hands. The solvent must be appropriate for the composition of the paint.

ACRYLIC PAINT: Pigment is combined with an acrylic polymer vehicle that is created in a laboratory. By itself, acrylic paint dries rapidly. Several different mediums can be used with acrylic paint: Retarder slows the drying process, flow extender thins the paint, an impasto medium thickens the paint, a gloss medium makes it shiny, a matte medium makes it dull.

Acrylic paint has been popular since the 1960s. Many artists like its versatility and the wide range of colors. Acrylic paint is also appreciated because its solvent is water, which is nonhazardous.

GOUACHE, 36: An opaque form of watercolor, which is also called tempera.

OIL PAINT, 14, 16, 20, 22, 24, 26, 28, 30, 32, 34, 38, 40, 44: Pigment is combined with an oil vehicle (usually linseed or poppy oil). The medium chosen by most artists is linseed oil. The solvent is turpentine. Oil paint dries slowly, which enables the artist to work on a painting for a long time. Some painters mix other materials, such as pumice or marble dust, into oil paint to produce thick layers of color. Oil paint is never mixed with water. Oil paint has been used since the fifteenth century. Until the early nineteenth century, artists or their assistants ground the pigment and combined the ingredients of paint in their studios. When the flexible tin tube (like a toothpaste tube) was invented in 1840, paint made by art suppliers became available.

TEMPERA: Pigment is combined with a water-based vehicle. The paint is combined with raw egg yolk to "temper" it into a mayonnaiselike consistency usable with a brush. The solvent for tempera is water. Tempera was used by the ancient Greeks and was the favorite method of painters during the medieval period in Europe. It is now available in tubes, ready to use. The painter supplies the egg yolk.

WATERCOLOR, 8, 36, 42: Pigment is combined with gum arabic, a water-based vehicle. Water is both the medium and the solvent. Watercolor paint now comes ready to use in tubes (moist) or in cakes (dry). With transparent watercolor, unlike other painting techniques, white paint is not used to lighten the colors. Watercolor paint is thinned with water, and areas of paper are often left uncovered to produce highlights.

Watercolor paint was first used 37,000 years ago by cave dwellers who created the first wall paintings.

PASTEL, 32: (1) A soft crayon made of powdered pigment, chalk, water, and mixed with a small amount of gum. (2) A painting or sketch made with this type of crayon.

PATRON, 14: One who supports the arts or an individual artist.

Paul Helleu Sketching with His Wife, 32

PERSPECTIVE: A method of representing people, places, and things in a painting or drawing to make them appear solid or three-dimensional, rather than flat. Six basic rules of perspective are used in Western art.

1. People in a painting appear larger when near and gradually become smaller as they get farther away.
2. People in the foreground overlap the activity behind them.
3. People become closer together as they get farther away.
4. People in the distance appear higher up in the picture than those in the foreground.
5. Colors are brighter and shadows are stronger in the foreground. Colors and shadows are paler and softer in the background.
6. Lines that, in real life, are parallel (such as the line of a ceiling and the line of a floor) are drawn at an angle, and the lines meet at the "horizon line," which represents the eye level of the artist and the viewer.

In addition, a special technique of perspective, called *foreshortening*, is used to compensate for distortion in figures and objects painted on a flat surface. For example, an artist will paint the hand of an outstretched arm larger than it is in proportion to the arm, which becomes smaller as it recedes toward the shoulder. This correction, necessary in a picture using perspective, is automatically made by the human eye observing a scene in life. *Foreshortening* refers to the representation of figures or objects, while *perspective* refers to the representation of a scene or a space.

Painters have used these methods to depict objects in space since the fifteenth century. But many twentieth-century artists have decided not to use perspective. An artist might emphasize color, line, or shape to express an idea, instead of showing people or objects in a realistic space.

Pianist and Checkers Players, 38

Picasso, Pablo, 36

PORTRAIT, 10, 12, 14, 20, 22, 26, 30, 32, 36: A painting, drawing, sculpture, or photograph that represents an individual's appearance and, often, his or her personality.

Portrait of the Emperor Maximilian I and His Family, 12

Renoir, Pierre-Auguste (Pronounced Ruhn-war), 26, 30, 32

Rubens, Peter Paul, 14

Rubens, His Wife Hélèna Fourment and Their Son Peter Paul, 14

Sargent, John Singer, 32

Schuffenecker Family, The, 34

SELF-PORTRAIT, 16: A portait of the artist created by the artist.

SHADING, 40, 42: The use of gradually darker and lighter colors to make an object appear solid and three-dimensional.

Six Studies for Family Group, 42

SKETCH, 28, 32: A quickly made drawing.

STILL LIFE, 26: A painting, drawing, or photograph of a group of objects.

Strigel, Bernhard, 12

TONE, 14, 18, 30: The sensation of an overall coloration in a painting. For example, an artist might begin by painting the entire picture in shades of greenish gray. After more colors are applied using transparent glazes, shadows, and highlights, the mass of greenish gray color underneath will show through and create an even tone, or "tonal harmony."

One of the ways that painters working with opaque colors can achieve the same effect is by adding one color, such as green, to every other color on their palette. This makes all of the colors seem more alike, or "harmonious." The effect of tonal harmony is part of the artist's vision and begins with the first brush strokes. It cannot be added to a finished painting.

TRANSPARENT, 14, 28: Allowing light to pass through so colors underneath can be seen. (The opposite of Opaque.)

TROMPE L'OEIL, 10: A technique used to paint a scene so realistically that the viewer may be tricked into thinking that people and objects in the picture are real—that the flat surface of the painting is an actual space. In sixteenth- and seventeenth-century Italian art, this technique was often used to create the illusion of soaring domes and arches in rooms with flat ceilings. (See also PERSPECTIVE.)

TURPENTINE: A strong-smelling solvent made from pine sap; used in oil painting. (See PAINT: OIL PAINT.)

Velázquez, Diego Rodríguez de Silva (Pronounced Veh-lass-kez), 16, 18

Credits

Frontispiece
THE GUILLON-LETHIERE FAMILY, 1815
Jean-Auguste-Dominique Ingres, French (1780–1867)
Pencil drawing

Page
9 *FAMILY SCENE*, c. 1150 B.C.
Tomb of Inherkhan
Unknown Egyptian artist
Borromeo/Art Resource, New York

11 *FAMILY AND COURT OF LUDOVICO III GONZAGA*, 1474
Andrea Mantegna, Italian
Mantua, Palazzo Ducale (Camera degli Sposi)
Scala/Art Resource, New York

13 *PORTRAIT OF THE EMPEROR MAXIMILIAN I
AND HIS FAMILY*, 1515
Bernhard Strigel, German
Kunsthistorisches Museum, Vienna
Nimatallah/Art Resource, New York

14 *HELENA FOURMENT*, c. 1632
Peter Paul Rubens, Flemish
Black, white, and red chalk , 19$^{1/2}$ x 12$^{4/5}$
Museum Boymans van Beuningen, Rotterdam

15 *RUBENS, HIS WIFE HELENA FOURMENT AND THEIR SON
PETER PAUL*, c. 1639
Peter Paul Rubens, Flemish
The Metropolitan Museum of Art, Gift of Mr. and Mrs. Charles Wrightsman, in
honor of Sir John Pope-Hennessy, 1981 (1981.238)

17/19 *THE MAIDS OF HONOR*, 1656
Diego Rodríguez de Silva Velázquez, Spanish
© Museo del Prado, Madrid

20 *STUDY FOR A GROUP OF FIGURES*
Thomas Gainsborough, English
Black and white chalks on toned paper
Courtesy New York Society Library

21 *THE BRIDGES FAMILY*, 1804
John Constable, English
Tate Gallery, London
Tate Gallery, London/Art Resource, New York

23 *THE BELLELLI FAMILY*, 1858–67
Edgar Degas, French
Musée D'Orsay, Paris © Photo R.M.N.

25 *LUNCHEON ON THE GRASS*, 1866
Claude Monet, French
Musée D'Orsay, Paris © Photo R.M.N.

27 *FAMILY REUNION*, 1865–69
Jean-Frédéric Bazille, French
Musée D'Orsay, Paris © Photo R.M.N.

28 *JULIE, CAT, AND BACKGROUND*, 1887
Pierre-Auguste Renoir, French
Crayon on paper, 24 x 18$^{1/4}$"
Private collection

29 *THE MONET FAMILY IN THEIR GARDEN*, 1874
Edouard Manet, French
The Metropolitan Museum of Art, Bequest of Joan Whitney Payson, 1975
(1976.201.14)

30 *THE ARTIST'S FAMILY*
Pierre-Auguste Renoir, French
Photograph © 1992 by The Barnes Foundation

31 *MADAME CHARPENTIER AND HER CHILDREN, GEORGETTE
AND PAUL*, 1878
Pierre-Auguste Renoir, French
The Metropolitan Museum of Art, Wolfe Fund, 1907. Catharine Lorrilard Wolfe
Collection. (07.122)

33 *PAUL HELLEU SKETCHING WITH HIS WIFE*, 1889
John Singer Sargent, American
The Brooklyn Museum Accession # 20.640
Museum Collection Fund

34 *MOTHER AND CHILD*
Mary Cassatt, American
Lithograph
Courtesy Isselbacher Gallery, New York

35 *THE SCHUFFENECKER FAMILY*, 1889
Paul Gauguin, French
Musée D'Orsay, Paris Photo: © R. M. N.

36 *MOTHER AND CHILD*, 1901
Pablo Picasso, Spanish
Harvard University Art Museums # 1951.57
Bequest—Collection of Maurice Wertheim, Class of 1906

37 *THE FAMILY OF ACROBATS WITH APE*, 1905
Pablo Picasso, Spanish
Göeteborg Konstmuseum, Sweden. Photo: Ebbe Carlson

38 *THE MUSIC LESSON — THE ARTIST'S FAMILY*, 1917
Henri Matisse, French
Oil on canvas, 96 x 82$^{1/2}$"
Photograph © 1992 by The Barnes Foundation

39 *PIANIST AND CHECKER PLAYERS*, 1924
Henri Matisse, French
National Gallery of Art, Washington, D.C.
Collection of Mr. and Mrs. Paul Mellon

40 *STUDY FOR MOTHER AND CHILD*, 1924
Fernand Léger, French
© 52-61-69 Philadelphia Museum of Art: The A.E. Gallation Collection

41 *HOMMAGE A LOUIS DAVID*, 1948–49
Fernand Léger, French
Musee National d'Art Moderne, Paris

43 *SIX STUDIES FOR FAMILY GROUP*, 1948
Henry Moore, English
© By kind permission of the Henry Moore Foundation

44 *MOTHER AND CHILD*, 1960
Jacques-Richard Chery, Haitian
Oil on Masonite, 22$^{1/4}$ x 26"
Milwaukee Art Museum, gift of Richard and Erna Flagg

45 *HAITIAN FAMILY*, 1962
Castera Bazile, Haitian
Milwaukee Art Museum, lent by Gabrielle Flagg Pfeiffer